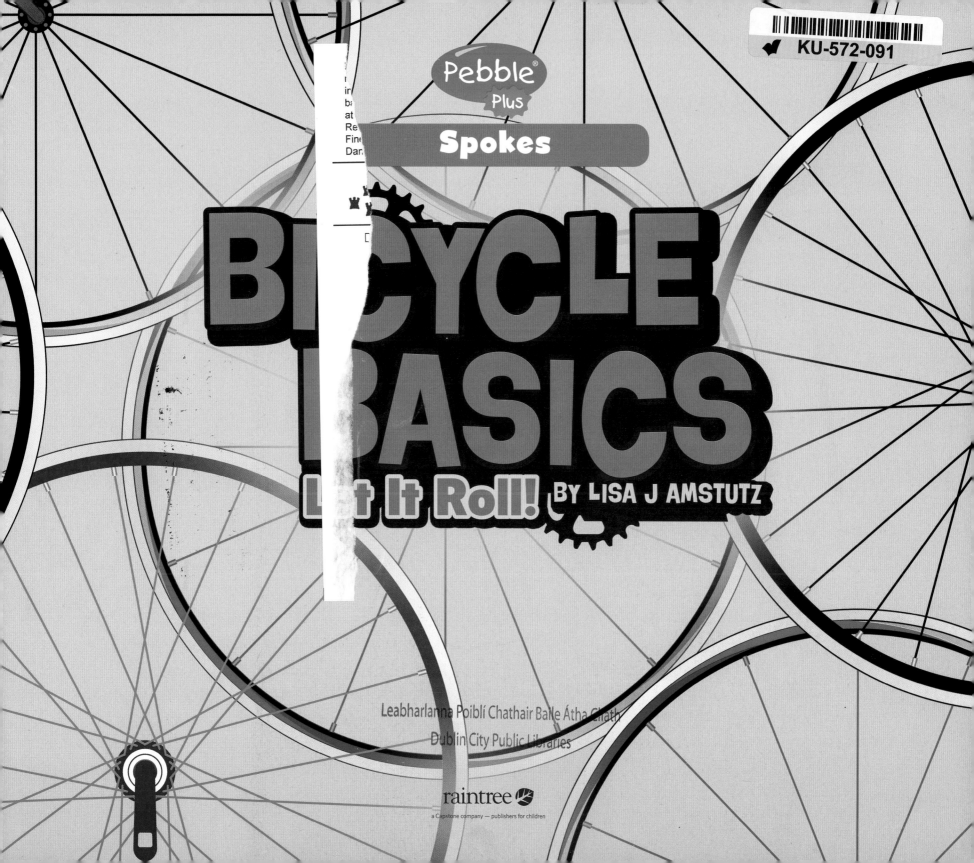

Pebble® Plus

**Spokes**

# BICYCLE BASICS

## Let It Roll! BY LISA J AMSTUTZ

raintree
a Capstone company — publishers for children

Raintree is an imprint of Capstone Global Library Limited, a company incorporated in England and Wales having its registered office at 264 Banbury Road, Oxford, OX2 7DY – Registered company number: 6695582

www.raintree.co.uk
myorders@raintree.co.uk

Edited by Jeni Wittrock
Designed by Kyle Grenz
Production by Jennifer Walker
Picture research by Sarah Schuette
Photo Schedule by Marcy Morin
Production by Capstone Global Library Ltd
Printed and bound in India.

ISBN 978 1 4747 3369 4 (hardback)
20 19 18 17 16
10 9 8 7 6 5 4 3 2 1

ISBN 978 1 4747 3374 8 (paperback)
21 20 19 18 17
10 9 8 7 6 5 4 3 2 1

**British Library Cataloguing in Publication Data**
A full catalogue record for this book is available from the British Library.

**Acknowledgements**
We would like to thank the following for permission to reproduce photographs: Capstone Studio: Karon Dubke, cover; Corbis: Tom Stewart, 5, Dreamstime: Brad Calkins, 17; Newscom: World History Archive, 13; Shutterstock: fotum, 15, Hodag Media, 11, homydesign, 7, Jean-Michel Girard, 20, Monkey Business Images, 19, 21; Wikimedia: Lokilech, 9

**Design Elements**
Shutterstock: filip robert, Kalmatsuy Tatyana

We would like to thank Gail Saunders-Smith for her invaluable help in the preparation of this book.

Every effort has been made to contact copyright holders of material reproduced in this book. Any omissions will be rectified in subsequent printings if notice is given to the publisher.

All the internet addresses (URLs) given in this book were valid at the time of going to press. However, due to the dynamic nature of the internet, some addresses may have changed, or sites may have changed or ceased to exist since publication. While the author and publisher regret any inconvenience this may cause readers, no responsibility for any such changes can be accepted by either the author or the publisher.

# Contents

# Let's ride!

Have somewhere to go?
Ride a bike! Bikes do not
pollute the air like cars do.
Cycling is good exercise too.
Most of all, cycling is fun.

Bikes come in many shapes and sizes. Some bikes are for racing. Others are for jumps and tricks. But bikes weren't always easy to use.

# The history of bicycles

The first bicycle was invented in 1817. It had two wheels but no pedals. The word bicycle means "two-wheel".

Pedals were added in 1839.
Early pedal bikes were hard
to ride. Some were very tall.
If riders fell off, they often
got hurt.

In 1885 JK Starley built the safety bicycle. A chain turned its wheels. Today's bikes are faster and lighter. But they work the same way.

13

# How a bike works

To ride a bike, push the pedals with your feet.
The pedals turn a large cog and chain. The chain turns the back wheel. Off you go!

pedal

cog

chain

A bike's rubber tyres wrap

around metal rims.

Tyres make rides less bumpy.

The hubs and spokes give

bike wheels strength.

rubber tyre

hub

spoke

To steer a bike, turn

the handlebars. Use the

brakes to stop or slow down.

Done cycling? When you

park, put down the kickstand.

# Bike safety

It is important to ride safely. Follow traffic rules. When you want to stop or turn, use hand signals. Always wear a helmet, and have fun!

**hand signals**

left    right    slow or stop

# Glossary

**brake** tool that slows down or stops a bike

**cog** toothed wheel

**handlebar** part of a bicycle that the rider holds on to and uses to steer

**hand signal** special sign to show others that you plan to stop or turn

**hub** centre part of a wheel

**invent** think up and make something new

**kickstand** piece of metal that sticks out to balance a parked bicycle

**pedal** lever on a bicycle that riders push with their feet

**pollute** make something dirty or unsafe

**rim** metal circle inside the tyre

**spoke** bar that goes out from the centre of the wheel to support the rim

**strength** quality of being strong

**tyre** ring of rubber on the outside of a wheel; a tube of air fits inside

**traffic** vehicles that are moving on a road

# Read more

*Amazing Bike Tricks* (Try This at Home), Ellen Labrecque (Raintree, 2013)

*Being Safe on a Bike* (Keep Yourself Safe), Honor Head (Franklin Watts, 2015)

*Bike: In 10 Simple Steps* (How to Design the World's Best), Paul Mason (Wayland, 2016)

# Websites

www.bbc.co.uk/radio4/history/making_history/makhist10_prog9d.shtml
This BBC website provides a history of bicycles.

www.dkfindout.com/uk/sports/cycling
Discover lots of facts about bikes and cycling on the DK Find Out! website.

# Index